For Jason
with love
from
Aunty Mary Uncle Stuart
Katie & Harry xx

XMAS 2007

Transformers Annual 2008
First published in Great Britain by HarperCollins Children's Books in 2007
3 5 7 9 10 8 6 4 2

978-0-00-725109-4
0-00-725109-2

A CIP catalogue record for this title is available from the British Library.
No part of this publication may be reproduced, stored in a retrieval system or transmitted in any form
or by any means, electronic, mechanical, photocopying, recording or otherwise, without the prior
permission of HarperCollins Publishers Ltd, 77-85 Fulham Palace Road, Hammersmith, London W6 8JB.
The HarperCollins website address is: www.harpercollinschildrensbooks.co.uk

Printed and bound in Spain

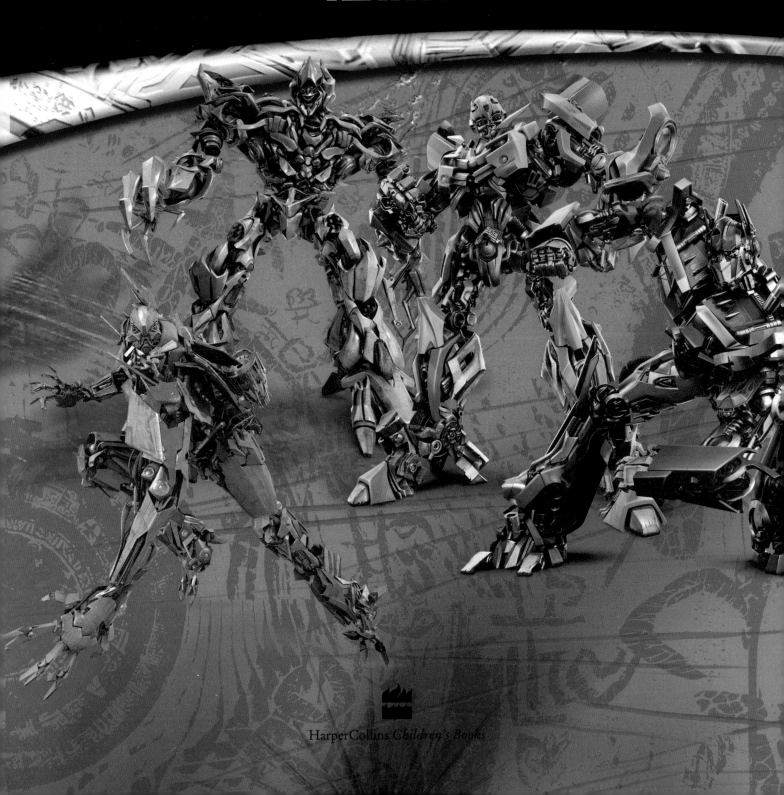

TRANS FORMERS

ANNUAL 2008

HarperCollins Children's Books

CONTENTS

Long ago, an alien race called Transformers fought over a precious substance on a distant planet. They battled over the Allspark—the source of the aliens' life force.

When wars destroyed the planet, the only remaining Allspark was lost. It flew through space, a mysterious group of numbers running across its surface, until it was drawn to another planet. . . .

Years later, Captain Archibald Witwicky was exploring in the Arctic when he fell through a hole in the snow.

What he saw underground changed his life forever. Buried in the ice was a giant metallic man! The captain chipped away at some ice to get a closer look, which somehow activated the figure. Suddenly a white-hot laser blast shot out of its eyes!

The captain's eyeglasses cracked and flew to the ground, but not before they were etched forever with an alien code. It was the same group of numbers that covered the Allspark.

No one ever believed the captain. The outlandish tale made everyone think he was insane.

Still, generations later, he was the best ancestor that Sam Witwicky could come up with for his high school report on family history. The captain's great-great-grandson showed his class the Arctic explorer's tools and said he planned to sell them. As usual, nobody was interested in what Sam had to say.

But things were about to change. After school, Sam's dad was taking him to buy a car. Once he had his own wheels, even pretty Mikaela Banes would notice him. Or so he daydreamed. . . .

A salesman moved in on them right away. He wrapped his arm around Sam and said, "Drivers don't pick their cars! Cars pick their drivers. It's a mystical bond between man and machine."

The cars on the lot were dented and rusted, not at all what Sam had in mind. There was a yellow Camaro with black racing stripes that didn't seem *so* bad.

The salesman steered Sam toward some other cars. But when Sam stepped out of the Camaro, its horn honked furiously. It was as if the Camaro really *had* chosen Sam!

Meanwhile, on the other side of the world, a group of soldiers had just flown back to their army base in the desert when a special-ops chopper touched down beside them.

The pilot was a mustached man. When the soldiers ordered him to step out, he flickered like a hologram and vanished!

A shrill shriek came from the chopper, jolting all the electronic systems at the base with a pulse of pure energy. Then, before the soldiers' eyes, it began changing!

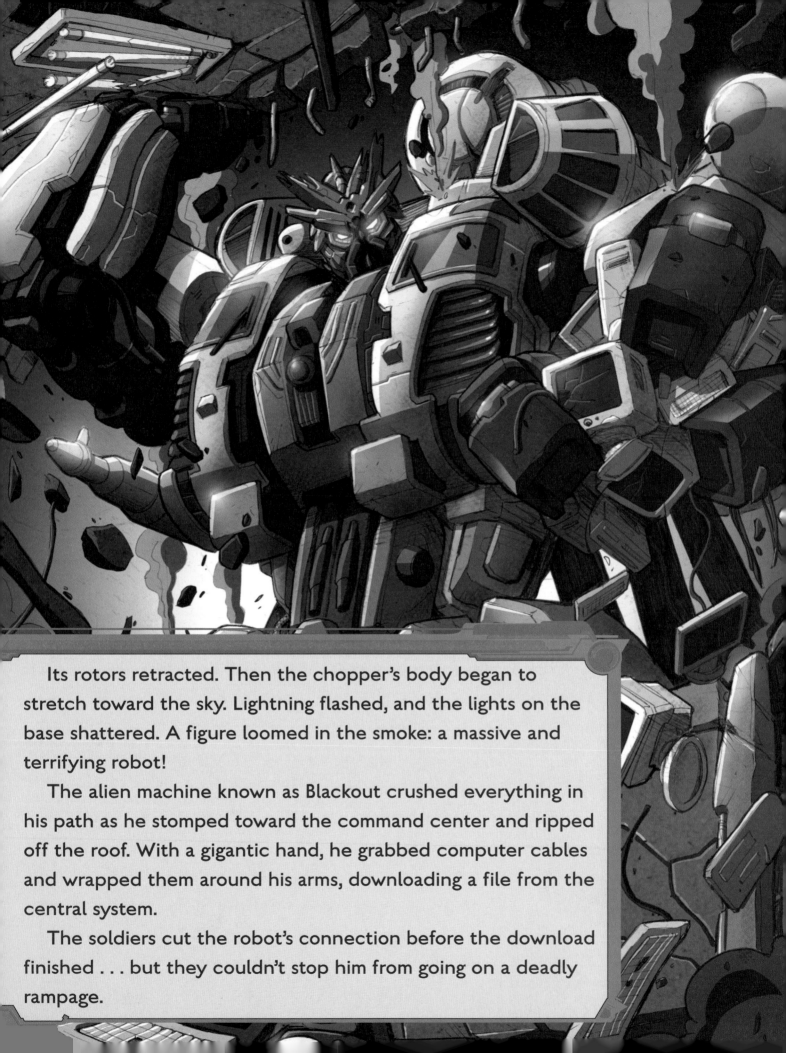

Its rotors retracted. Then the chopper's body began to stretch toward the sky. Lightning flashed, and the lights on the base shattered. A figure loomed in the smoke: a massive and terrifying robot!

The alien machine known as Blackout crushed everything in his path as he stomped toward the command center and ripped off the roof. With a gigantic hand, he grabbed computer cables and wrapped them around his arms, downloading a file from the central system.

The soldiers cut the robot's connection before the download finished . . . but they couldn't stop him from going on a deadly rampage.

In Washington, top officials learned of the attack. "It hacked our military network," explained the Secretary of Defense. "We aren't sure exactly what it was after, but we assume it'll try again."

The government's best hope for solving the mystery was a young analyst named Maggie Marconi. They brought her in immediately.

On Air Force One, the president had also been informed of the situation. Little did he know that another attack was about to happen in his own plane!

Nestled under a seat, a small radio began to stir, then sprouted arms and legs, and transformed into a robot! The Transformer known as Frenzy sneaked around and located a computer. Then he downloaded the same file that Blackout had tried to steal from the base.

From her new desk at the Pentagon, Maggie noticed that both hackers were after the same thing. She also noticed that Frenzy had planted a virus. Her superiors argued over who had done it—and why. "Russia and China are the only countries with this kind of capability," one admiral said firmly.

Maggie had a hunch that something else was going on. But nobody listened when she said, "There's more to this than meets the eye. I *know* it."

As soon as she could, Maggie tracked down her friend Glen. Together, they listened to a recording of a weird sound the hackers had made.

"The signal strength is through the roof," Glen noted.

"It hacked the Pentagon in less than a minute," said Maggie.

Glen drew in his breath. "That's impossible," he replied. "It'd be . . . real Artificial Intelligence."

Maggie feared the same thing herself. But could there really be alien machines on Earth?

The Secret Service was scouring Air Force One for clues. But Frenzy dropped out of the plane unseen and sped over to a waiting police car.

On a computer inside the police car, Frenzy found what he was looking for: the captain's glasses for sale online. And the seller's name and photograph were displayed underneath! The next task would be to locate Sam Witwicky.

INCOMING!

The Transformers arrive on Earth!

MISTAKEN IDENTITY

When a Transformer lands in her backyard, a little girl thinks she's getting a special visit. Use the code below to find out who she thinks her visitor is!

A=Z B=Y C=X D=W E=V F=U G=T
H=S I=R J=Q K=P L=O M=N
N=M O=L P=K Q=J R=I S=H T=G U=F
V=E W=D X=C Y=B Z=A

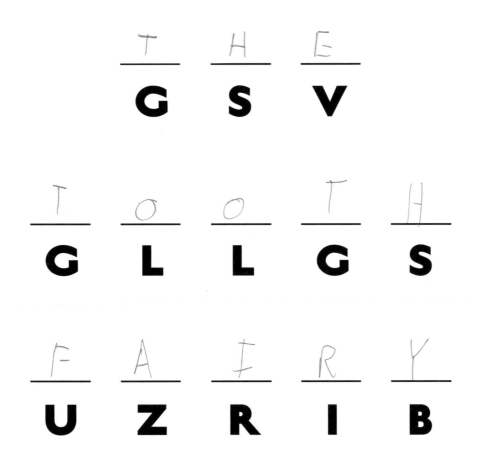

T H E
G S V

T O O T H
G L L G S

F A I R Y
U Z R I B

TRANSFORMERS CROSSWORD

Use the picture clues to fill in the crossword puzzle below.

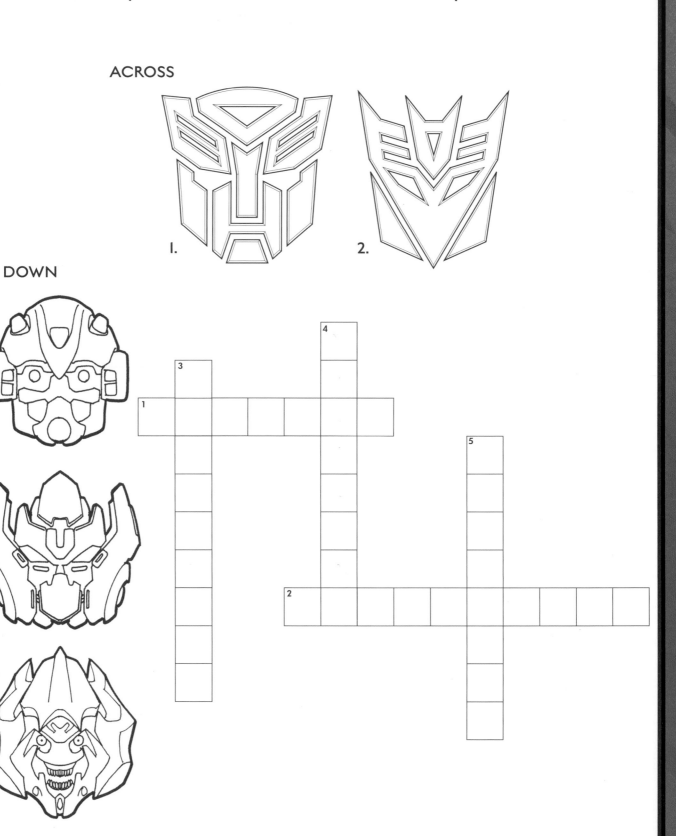

ACROSS

1.

2.

DOWN

3.

4.

5.

UNDER WRAPS

The U.S. government wants to keep the location of the Allspark a secret. Use the code below to find out where it's being hidden.

A   D   E   H   M   O   R   V

H _ O _ O _ V _ E _ R _

_ D _ A _ M

That night, Sam was half-asleep when he heard a sound in his driveway. When he looked out the window, he saw a strange mustached man driving off with his car!

Sam had waited way too long for a car. He wasn't about to let someone steal his Camaro. He ran outside and jumped on his bike. He followed the car across town and through the gate of an abandoned factory.

It was odd enough that the mustached man seemed to disappear into thin air. But then, before Sam's eyes, the Camaro shifted shape! Through the dense fog, Sam could tell his car—if he could still call it that—was walking on two legs! It pulled something from its chest . . . and then it beamed a bright light into the sky!

Before Sam could figure out what happened, the Camaro took off again.

The next morning, the car was parked out in front of Sam's home as if nothing had ever happened. Sam left on his bike for a friend's house. But when he looked around, the Camaro was following him!

Sam was so scared he kept right on pedaling, almost hitting Mikaela Banes.

"Hey! Watch it!" she shouted. She thought Sam was acting strangely, so she jumped on her scooter and followed him.

Sam headed for a parking lot, trying to lose the Camaro there. But he plowed into a police cruiser! Sam prepared to tell the officer about his crazy Camaro. Then something even stranger happened!

The cop car jumped forward and knocked Sam down. The cruiser's
headlights stretched out until they were inches away from Sam's frightened face.
Then, in seconds, the police car's doors tucked in, wheels disappeared, and
body morphed into an enormous sixteen-foot-tall robot . . . who pinned Sam to
a windshield!

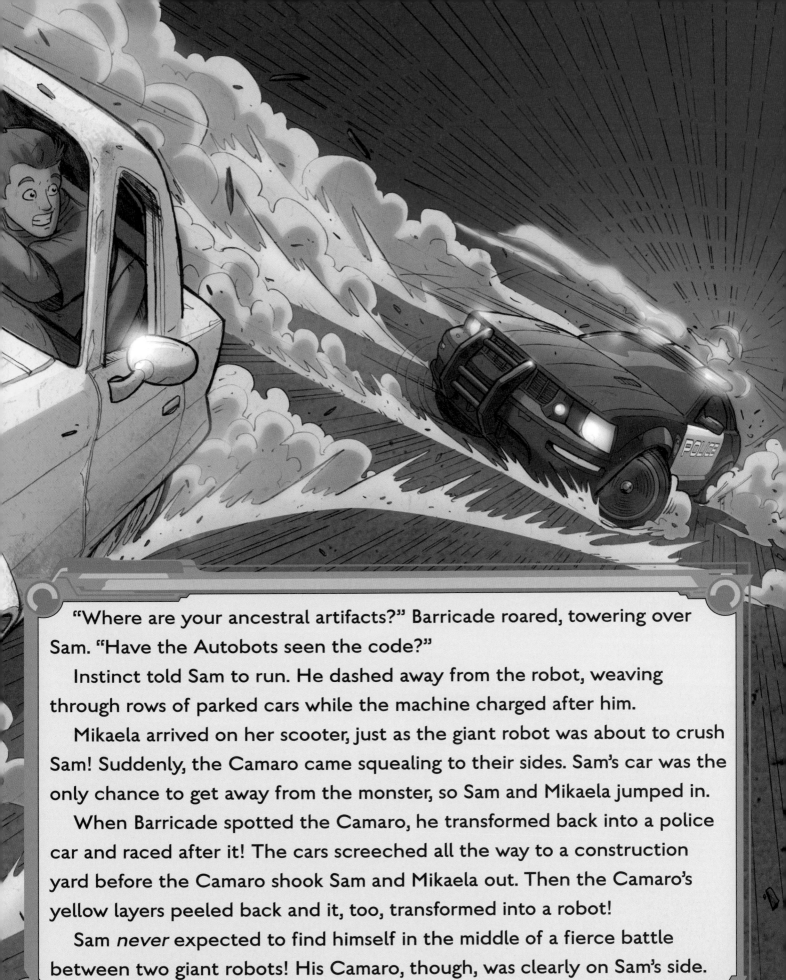

"Where are your ancestral artifacts?" Barricade roared, towering over Sam. "Have the Autobots seen the code?"

Instinct told Sam to run. He dashed away from the robot, weaving through rows of parked cars while the machine charged after him.

Mikaela arrived on her scooter, just as the giant robot was about to crush Sam! Suddenly, the Camaro came squealing to their sides. Sam's car was the only chance to get away from the monster, so Sam and Mikaela jumped in.

When Barricade spotted the Camaro, he transformed back into a police car and raced after it! The cars screeched all the way to a construction yard before the Camaro shook Sam and Mikaela out. Then the Camaro's yellow layers peeled back and it, too, transformed into a robot!

Sam *never* expected to find himself in the middle of a fierce battle between two giant robots! His Camaro, though, was clearly on Sam's side.

His new friend defeated the police car, and then turned to look at Sam. "I don't think he's gonna hurt us," Sam told Mikaela.

The robot transformed back into a car, his doors swinging open. Sam climbed in, needing to know what was going on.

Then the Camaro gave himself a makeover by scanning a newer Camaro parked on the street. He went from being a beat-up car to the very latest model!

Next, the Camaro drove up a hillside, where Sam and Mikaela could see meteors showering down to Earth. Hitting the ground, the spheres opened up like flowers.

Legs and arms emerged, followed by heads and faces. Then four silhouettes rose to their feet. The kids were watching some kind of alien invasion—of robots that towered over them!

One of the robots turned toward an eighteen-wheeler passing nearby, scanned it with a beam of light, and transformed himself into an identical truck. The others made themselves into a Search and Rescue vehicle, a pickup, and a luxury car!

Then they all reassumed robot forms. The eighteen-wheeler, seemingly the group's leader, began to speak.

"Samuel James Witwicky?" he asked.

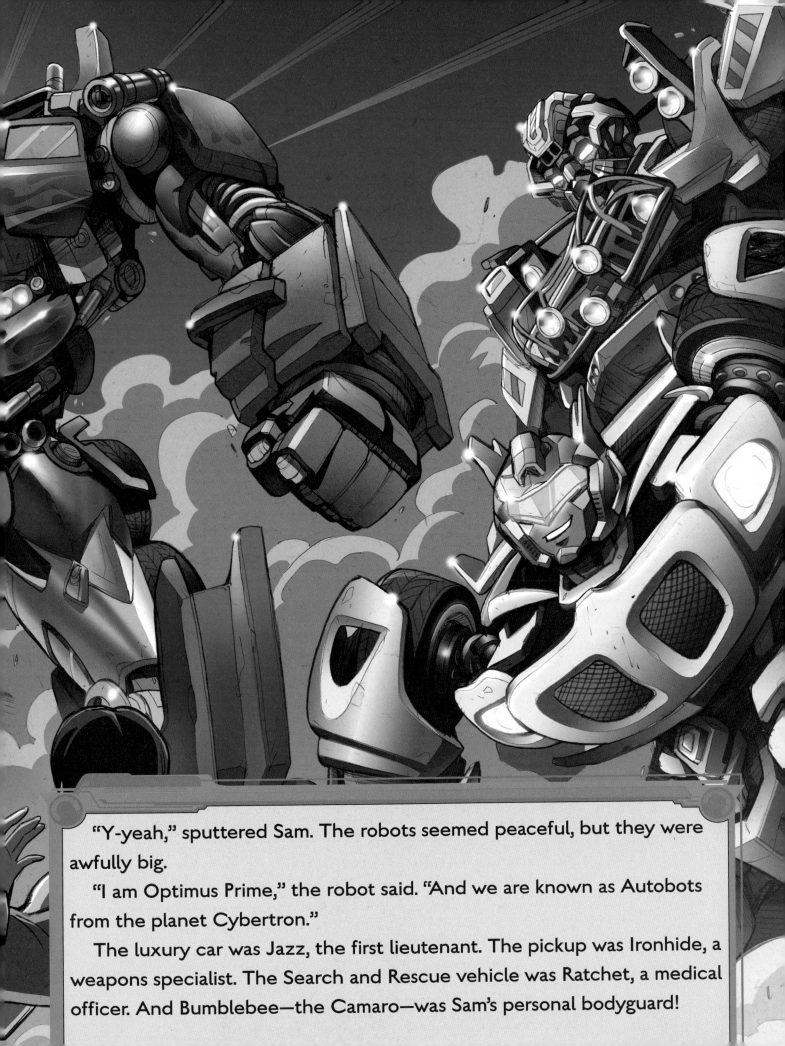

"Y-yeah," sputtered Sam. The robots seemed peaceful, but they were awfully big.

"I am Optimus Prime," the robot said. "And we are known as Autobots from the planet Cybertron."

The luxury car was Jazz, the first lieutenant. The pickup was Ironhide, a weapons specialist. The Search and Rescue vehicle was Ratchet, a medical officer. And Bumblebee—the Camaro—was Sam's personal bodyguard!

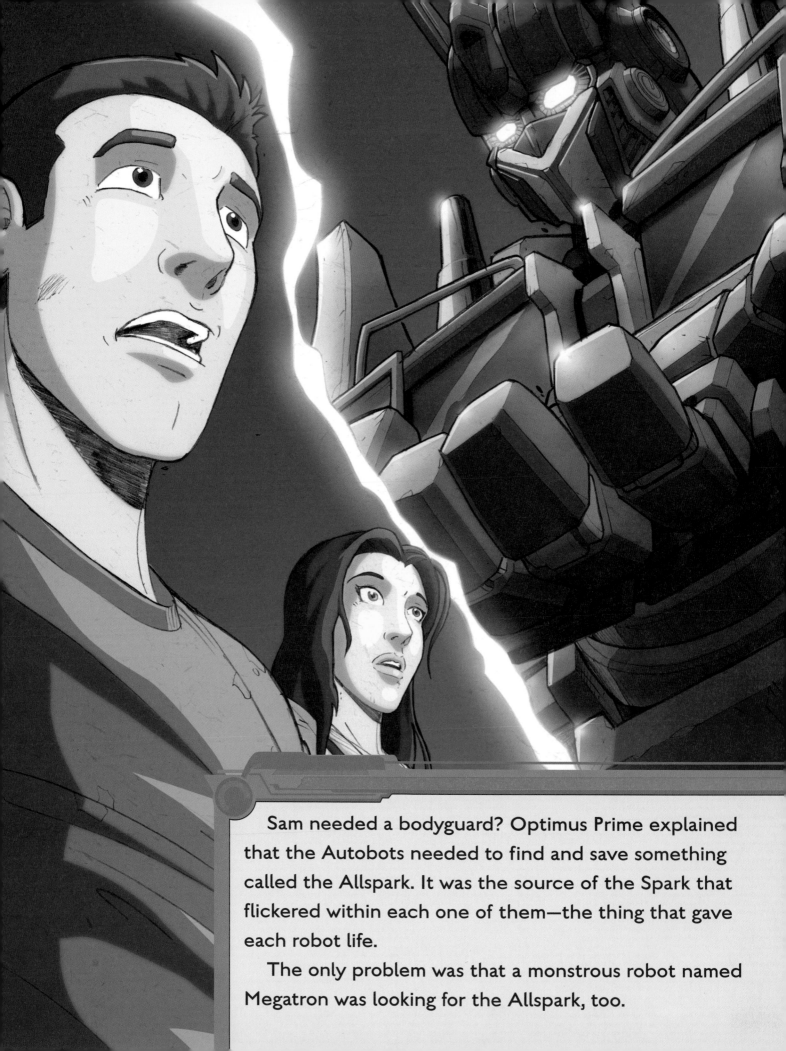

Sam needed a bodyguard? Optimus Prime explained that the Autobots needed to find and save something called the Allspark. It was the source of the Spark that flickered within each one of them—the thing that gave each robot life.

The only problem was that a monstrous robot named Megatron was looking for the Allspark, too.

Optimus Prime shook his head sadly. "Megatron and I are brothers. But he turned his armies against us, and for that betrayal they bear the name Decepticons."

Megatron's armies had all but destroyed their home planet.

"He followed the Allspark's signal here," Ironhide explained. "And then succumbed to the ice . . . where your ancestor encountered him."

Megatron's laser beam had etched the captain's glasses with a code—a map to the Allspark!

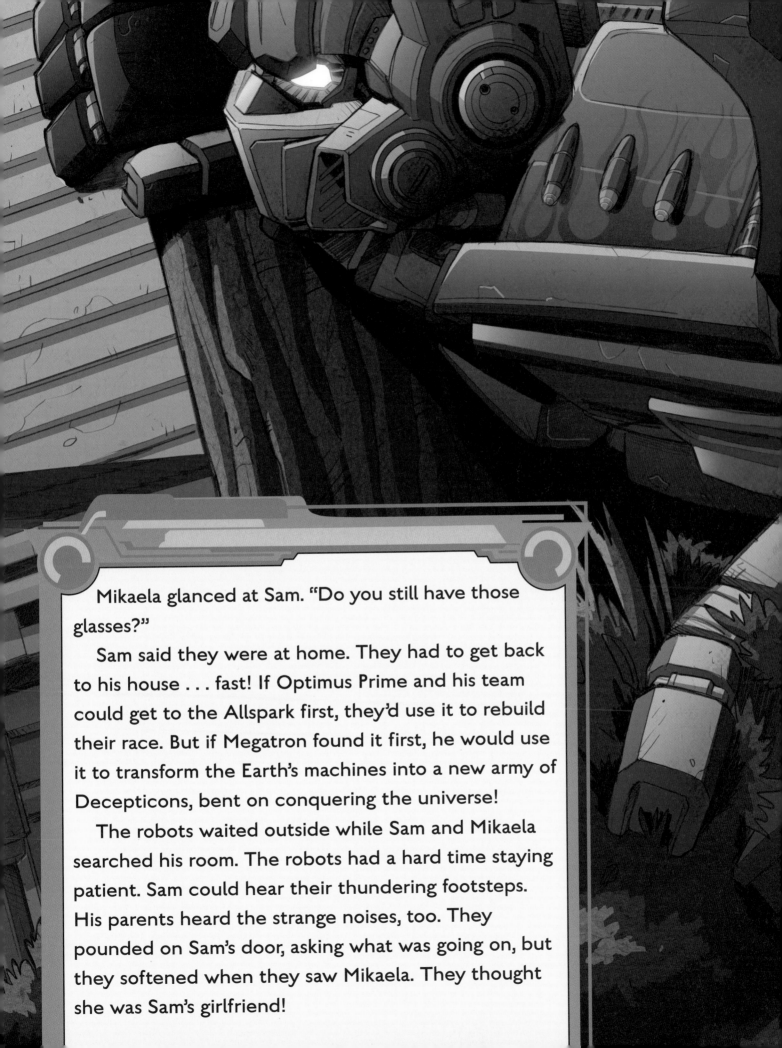

Mikaela glanced at Sam. "Do you still have those glasses?"

Sam said they were at home. They had to get back to his house . . . fast! If Optimus Prime and his team could get to the Allspark first, they'd use it to rebuild their race. But if Megatron found it first, he would use it to transform the Earth's machines into a new army of Decepticons, bent on conquering the universe!

The robots waited outside while Sam and Mikaela searched his room. The robots had a hard time staying patient. Sam could hear their thundering footsteps. His parents heard the strange noises, too. They pounded on Sam's door, asking what was going on, but they softened when they saw Mikaela. They thought she was Sam's girlfriend!

"By the way," Sam asked casually, "have you seen my backpack?"

"It's on the kitchen table," replied his mom.

Sam found it just as his father answered the ringing doorbell. Guys in suits were at the door. One of them flashed a badge. "We're with the government," Agent Simmons told Sam's dad. "Sector Seven. We believe your son is involved in a national security matter."

Before Sam could explain to the robots, he and Mikaela were forced into a big black SUV!

Optimus Prime and the Autobots appeared before the agents could question Sam. Their giant fingers crashed through the windows and peeled off the roof of the truck! The government agents didn't seem surprised by the robots. *What was Sector Seven, anyway?* Sam wondered.

Then Optimus Prime lifted Sam and Mikaela onto his shoulders and charged a fleet of trucks that was closing in. With one pulse blast, the robots flattened all their tires!

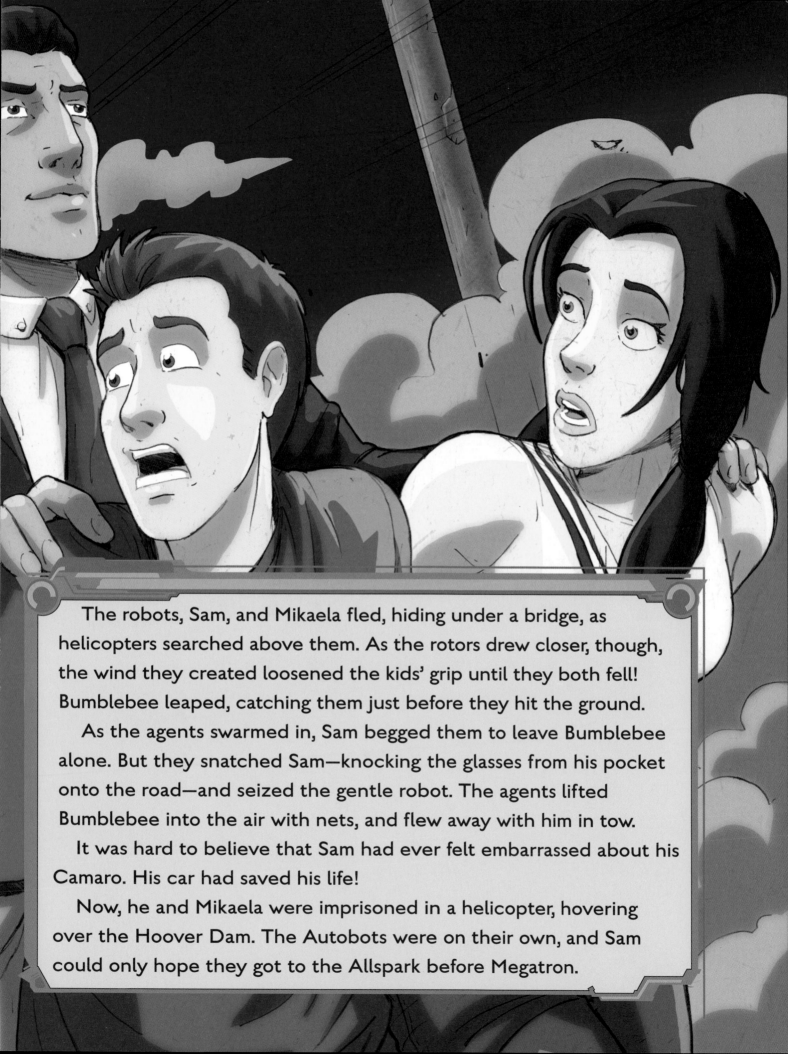

The robots, Sam, and Mikaela fled, hiding under a bridge, as helicopters searched above them. As the rotors drew closer, though, the wind they created loosened the kids' grip until they both fell! Bumblebee leaped, catching them just before they hit the ground.

As the agents swarmed in, Sam begged them to leave Bumblebee alone. But they snatched Sam—knocking the glasses from his pocket onto the road—and seized the gentle robot. The agents lifted Bumblebee into the air with nets, and flew away with him in tow.

It was hard to believe that Sam had ever felt embarrassed about his Camaro. His car had saved his life!

Now, he and Mikaela were imprisoned in a helicopter, hovering over the Hoover Dam. The Autobots were on their own, and Sam could only hope they got to the Allspark before Megatron.

TRANSFORMER LINGO

Transformers are more than just robots in disguise. Cross out the word "Transformer" every time it appears to reveal their special motto.

T R A N S F O R M E R M
O R E T R A N S F O R M
E R T R A N S F O R M E
R T H A N T R A N S F O
R M E R M E E T S T R A
N S F O R M E R T R A N
S F O R M E R T H E T R
A N S F O R M E R T R A
N S F O R M E R E Y E

_ _ _ _   _ _ _ _

_ _ _ _ _   _ _ _

_ _ _

42

WHO'S WHO

Search the puzzle below for the names of the Transformers, their friends, and their planet. The words are hidden reading forward, backward, up, down, or diagonally in either direction.

Barricade

Megatron

Optimus Prime

Ratchet

N	B	R	N	M	G	B	H	Z	E	L	O
O	O	L	A	N	M	S	S	D	R	P	J
R	F	R	T	T	G	X	I	Z	T	U	N
T	F	A	T	Y	C	H	E	I	B	Z	W
A	N	B	P	R	N	H	M	L	A	T	V
G	E	N	T	O	E	U	E	Z	R	K	W
E	W	G	R	Z	S	B	F	T	R	T	G
M	H	I	S	P	P	V	Y	E	I	E	N
T	T	A	R	M	L	S	B	C	C	Q	D
F	M	I	K	A	E	L	A	U	A	P	X
J	M	P	X	B	T	A	E	Z	D	C	P
E	E	E	B	E	L	B	M	U	B	E	P	Z

Bumblebee

Sam

Cybertron

Mikaela

Ironhide

In Washington, no one believed Maggie, thinking Russia or China was behind the attacks. And they were ready to strike back.

Defense Secretary Keller was looking at satellite images when a man rushed into his office with a briefcase, saying he was with an agency called Sector Seven. Keller had never heard of it. He was annoyed by the intrusion. Then all of his screens went black because of an uploaded virus, just as Maggie had predicted. And it had shut down satellite, cable, and cellular networks worldwide.

"Sir, you need to see what I have in my briefcase *now*," Agent Tom Banachek said to Keller. "Sector Seven secretly convened under President Hoover over eighty years ago, for one reason: Aliens are real," he explained. He showed Keller pictures of alien robots on Mars—and of Blackout in the desert, demolishing American troops.

"Are we talking about . . . an invasion?" Keller asked in disbelief.

Banachek nodded. "Something's coming.

Meanwhile, Optimus Prime found the glasses where Sam had dropped them. The alien code converted into a map that pinpointed the Allspark's location!

But Jazz wasn't ready to leave. "They took Bumblebee!" he cried. He wanted to avenge their friend.

"We aren't like the Decepticons. We never harm humans. Bumblebee would want us to complete our mission," Optimus Prime cautioned. With that, the Autobots transformed into vehicles and streaked down a desert highway.

Back in Sam's neighborhood, the police car known as Barricade staggered to his feet. With an eerie howl, he brought four lethal Decepticons out of hiding!

Starscream was an attack plane, and Brawl an army tank. Bonecrusher was a mine-clearing vehicle, and Blackout was the killer chopper that had already leveled the American military base. They headed to where they could find their leader . . . and the Allspark.

The Transformers would soon arrive at Hoover Dam. Sam and Mikaela were already there with the few other people who knew about the presence of aliens on Earth: Maggie and Glen, some government operatives, and the surviving soldiers from the desert base.

"Here's the situation," said Agent Banachek. "We're facing war against a technological civilization far superior to our own." With communications down, Banachek expected them to share what they knew. He was about to show what Sector Seven knew, too.

The group followed him into a brilliantly lit underground lab. It held a gargantuan robot, imprisoned in blocks of ice: Megatron, frozen since he landed in the Arctic.

But that wasn't Sector Seven's only surprise. In another room was the Allspark itself, constantly monitored from a sealed control room.

"President Hoover had the dam built around it," Banachek explained. That was because the Allspark's energy could transform even the smallest machine into a monster!

Maggie was the first to discover they were all in grave danger. On Air Force One, the Decepticons had gained access to the location of the Allspark . . . which meant they knew where it was *right now*!

Just then, the roar of gathering Decepticons began to shake the dam. The rumbling created cracks in the ice around Megatron! His eyes opened and his mind began to wake up slowly from his long sleep.

As the soldiers prepared for attack, Sam cried, "Wait a second! Take me to my car! He's a Transformer, and he can get the Allspark out of here!"

Bumblebee was laid out on a table when Sector Seven agents and Sam burst in. He seemed okay and patted Sam's head kindly. Together they turned to their important job.

Having just arrived at the dam, the other Autobots stood guard as Bumblebee kneeled in front of the Allspark. He sang to it until it folded up into a smaller shape, like a child's toy. Then Bumblebee transformed into his Camaro form, and Sam and Mikaela climbed in, securing the Allspark with seat belts. They sped away, followed by soldiers and the rest of the Autobots!

At the same moment, Megatron finally broke free. He transformed into a hypersonic alien jet and blasted through the dam that had imprisoned him! Ripping through the air, he met the other Decepticons at the top of the dam. "We are ready to transform the machines!" shrieked Starscream.

That's when Megatron noticed Bumblebee driving toward a city. His X-ray vision revealed the Allspark hidden inside.

But before the Decepticons could reach Bumblebee, Optimus Prime began a robot-on-robot attack. Ironhide flipped over a truck to shield the kids. But a blast from Starscream split the truck in two, knocking Bumblebee backward . . . and cutting the Allspark loose from his back seat!

Injured, Bumblebee crawled toward the Allspark to protect it. The Autobots held their own for a little while . . . until Jazz was hit by a massive pulse from Megatron.

Optimus Prime surged toward Megatron, ready to face him.

Megatron glanced at the humans fighting alongside the Autobots and snarled. "Pathetic. You still make allies of the weak."

"Where you see weakness, I see strength," argued Optimus Prime.

"So be it, brother," said Megatron. "Our war begins again . . . on Earth!"

As the two collided, Sam clutched the Allspark. Knowing the soldiers had radioed for help, he decided to signal a chopper from a nearby roof and get the Allspark out of the city.

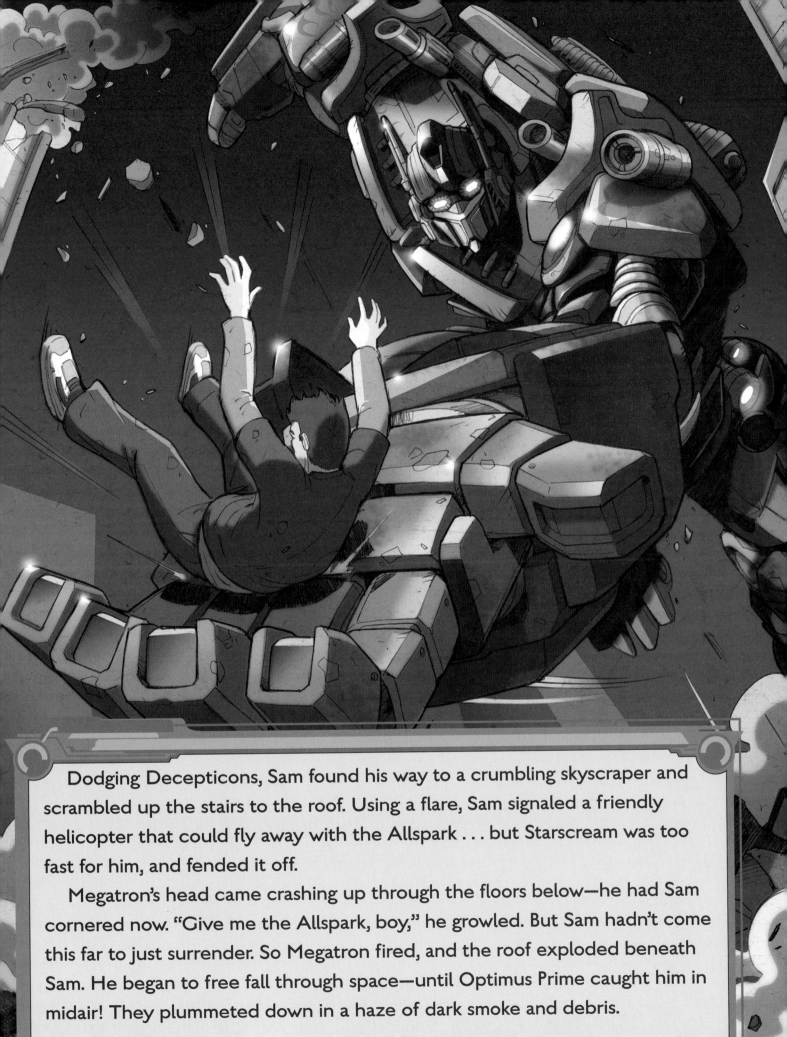

Dodging Decepticons, Sam found his way to a crumbling skyscraper and scrambled up the stairs to the roof. Using a flare, Sam signaled a friendly helicopter that could fly away with the Allspark . . . but Starscream was too fast for him, and fended it off.

Megatron's head came crashing up through the floors below—he had Sam cornered now. "Give me the Allspark, boy," he growled. But Sam hadn't come this far to just surrender. So Megatron fired, and the roof exploded beneath Sam. He began to free fall through space—until Optimus Prime caught him in midair! They plummeted down in a haze of dark smoke and debris.

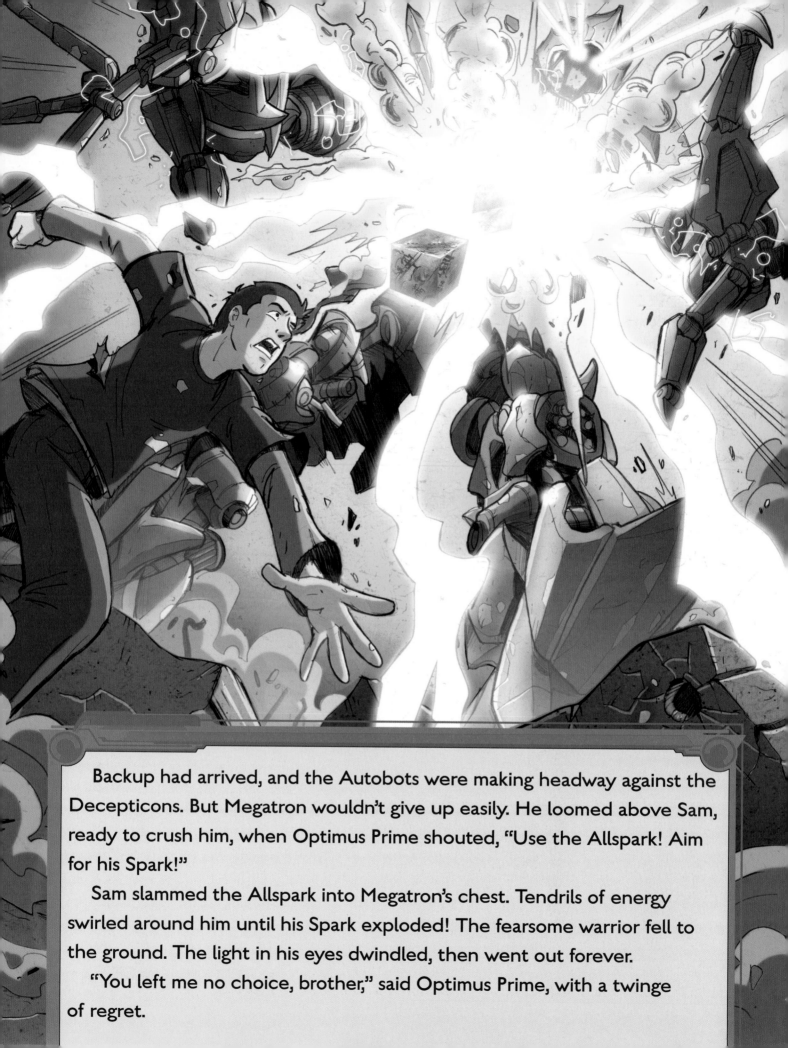

Backup had arrived, and the Autobots were making headway against the Decepticons. But Megatron wouldn't give up easily. He loomed above Sam, ready to crush him, when Optimus Prime shouted, "Use the Allspark! Aim for his Spark!"

Sam slammed the Allspark into Megatron's chest. Tendrils of energy swirled around him until his Spark exploded! The fearsome warrior fell to the ground. The light in his eyes dwindled, then went out forever.

"You left me no choice, brother," said Optimus Prime, with a twinge of regret.

Suddenly Sam realized something terrible. He had won the battle by destroying the Allspark. Without its life force, his friends would be the last of their kind, unable to repopulate their planet as they'd planned. Sam looked up at Optimus.

Optimus Prime was sorrowful but determined. "We will survive," he said. "We must. For those who did not."

Sam was determined to survive, too. Back at school, he held his head up with more confidence than he ever had before. And it didn't hurt that Mikaela, spotting him in the hallway for the first time after their adventure, rushed up and gave him the biggest hug of all time.

The Autobots were going to make a new home on Earth, and would be hiding in plain sight. Optimus Prime sent a message to his fellow Autobots still out in space. Looking up into the sky, he transmitted a call into the lonely universe: "To all surviving Autobots taking refuge among the stars. You are not alone. We are here. We are waiting."

WHAT IF . . .

If you could transform into any vehicle or object,
what would you be?
Would you be an Autobot or Decepticon?
Draw your new identity below.

VICTORY!

After a fierce struggle, Optimus Prime is badly hurt. Suddenly, Megatron's Spark is destroyed by the Allspark! Who used the Allspark to defeat Megatron? Cross out all the letters that are found in DECEPTICON to reveal the answer.

```
D  P  T  E  C  I  D  N  E  P
I  N  P  I  T  D  E  C  S  I
C  E  N  T  P  C  O  D  E  N
N  I  C  T  O  P  D  E  N  I
T  I  O  P  A  I  O  D  N  C
E  I  C  N  P  D  E  D  M  O
```

A PEACEFUL NEW HOME

The Autobots have a new home on planet Earth. There are many more Autobots living in far-off worlds that must now be summoned. Connect the dots to see who is calling out to those Transformers.